Vocal Selections

Aaron Harnick   David Broser   Triptyk Studios   Spencer B. Ross
Harbor Entertainment   Berkeley Repertory Theatre   Center Theatre Group
Simone Genatt Haft   Marc Routh   Saltaire Investment Group   The John Gore Organization
David Mirvish   Terry Schnuck
AND
Jujamcyn Theaters

T0071508

PRESENT

Amélie
a new musical

BOOK BY	MUSIC BY	LYRICS BY
CRAIG LUCAS	DANIEL MESSÉ	NATHAN TYSEN AND DANIEL MESSÉ

BASED ON THE MOTION PICTURE BY
Jean-Pierre Jeunet and Guillaume Laurant

STARRING

Phillipa Soo

Adam Chanler-Berat

WITH

Emily Afton   David Andino   Audrey Bennett   Randy Blair   Heath Calvert
Alison Cimmet   Savvy Crawford   Trey Ellett   Manoel Felciano   Harriett D. Foy   Alyse Alan Louis
Maria-Christina Oliveras   Destinee Rea   Jacob Keith Watson   Paul Whitty
AND
Tony Sheldon

SCENIC AND COSTUME DESIGN	LIGHTING DESIGN	SOUND DESIGN	PROJECTION DESIGN
David Zinn	Jane Cox & Mark Barton	Kai Harada	Peter Nigrini

PUPPET DESIGN	HAIR/WIG DESIGN	CREATIVE CONSULTANT
Amanda Villalobos	Charles G. LaPointe	Tony Taccone

VOCAL ARRANGEMENTS	CASTING BY	ORCHESTRATIONS	MUSIC COORDINATOR
Kimberly Grigsby & Daniel Messé	Jim Carnahan, C.S.A. Stephen Kopel, C.S.A.	Bruce Coughlin	Dean Sharenow

MARKETING DIRECTOR	ADVERTISING & MARKETING	PRESS
Nick Pramik	SpotCo	Polk & Co.

PRODUCTION STAGE MANAGER	COMPANY MANAGER	PRODUCTION MANAGEMENT	GENERAL MANAGEMENT
James Harker	Kimberly Shaw	Aurora Productions	Richards/Climan, Inc.

ASSOCIATE PRODUCERS
Lauren Heirigs, Stephanie Cowan, YL Entertainment & Sports Corp., Nelke Planning Co. Ltd, Disk Garage, Tsinghua Culture Media Corp.

MUSIC DIRECTOR
Kimberly Grigsby

MUSICAL STAGING AND CHOREOGRAPHY BY
Sam Pinkleton

DIRECTED BY
Pam MacKinnon

World premiere produced in September 2015 by Berkeley Repertory Theatre
Tony Taccone, Artistic Director   Susan Medak, Managing Director
Presented in December 2016 by Center Theatre Group
Michael Ritchie, Artistic Director, Stephen D. Rountree, Managing Director, Douglas C. Baker, Producing Director
The Producers wish to express their appreciation to the Theatre Development Fund for its support of this production.

Cover art courtesy of SpotCo

ISBN 978-1-4950-9978-6

Visit Hal Leonard Online at
www.halleonard.com

Contact us:
Hal Leonard
7777 West Bluemound Road
Milwaukee, WI 53213
Email: info@halleonard.com

In Europe, contact:
Hal Leonard Europe Limited
42 Wigmore Street
Marylebone, London, W1U 2RN
Email: info@halleonardeurope.com

In Australia, contact:
Hal Leonard Australia Pty. Ltd.
4 Lentara Court
Cheltenham, Victoria, 3192 Australia
Email: info@halleonard.com.au

TIMES ARE HARD FOR DREAMERS

Lyrics by NATHAN TYSEN and DANIEL MESSÉ
Music by DANIEL MESSÉ

past.

Off the train __ in Par - is, half __ a mile __ from Sac - re Coeur, the cit - y's

wak - ing up for me. A

sign says an __ a - part - ment's va - cant on the sec - ond floor __ and sud - den - ly __

THE GIRL WITH THE GLASS

Lyrics by NATHAN TYSEN and DANIEL MESSÉ
Music by DANIEL MESSÉ

each oth - er's eye, ___ but the girl with the glass ___ looks a -

AMÉLIE:

The girl with the glass. __

way.

The girl with the glass. __

I won - der what does she see? __

The girl with the glass.___

As if she's look - ing out at me....___

Just a

DUFAYEL:

young girl who does - n't___ be - long to an -

- y - where ___ or an - y - one. ___

Dictated

AMÉLIE:

May-be this whole soi-ree ___ is a par-ty ___ she's ___ thrown. May-be she's re-u-ni - ted that dog with its own - er. And may-be she ___ whis-pered that he's in-to him, ___ while she sits there and watch-es ___ it ___ all from the rim of ___ her ___ glass. ___

poco accel.

a tempo

TOUR DE FRANCE

Lyrics by NATHAN TYSEN and DANIEL MESSÉ
Music by DANIEL MESSÉ

AMÉLIE:
Sir, may I lend a hand? May I take your cane? Care-ful of the curb, here we go. ___ Put a-way your cup. Turn-ing down the lane, lis-ten to the squeak of the bak-er-y cart ___ leav-ing a

three mel - on slic - es _____ deep. As

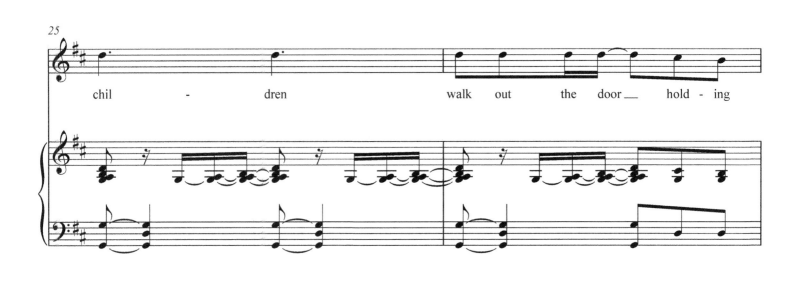

chil - dren walk out the door ___ hold - ing

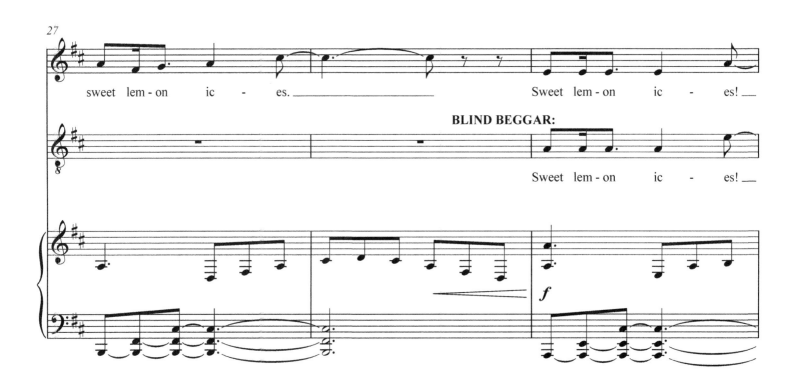

sweet lem - on ic - es. _____ Sweet lem - on ic - es! ___

BLIND BEGGAR:

Sweet lem - on ic - es! ___

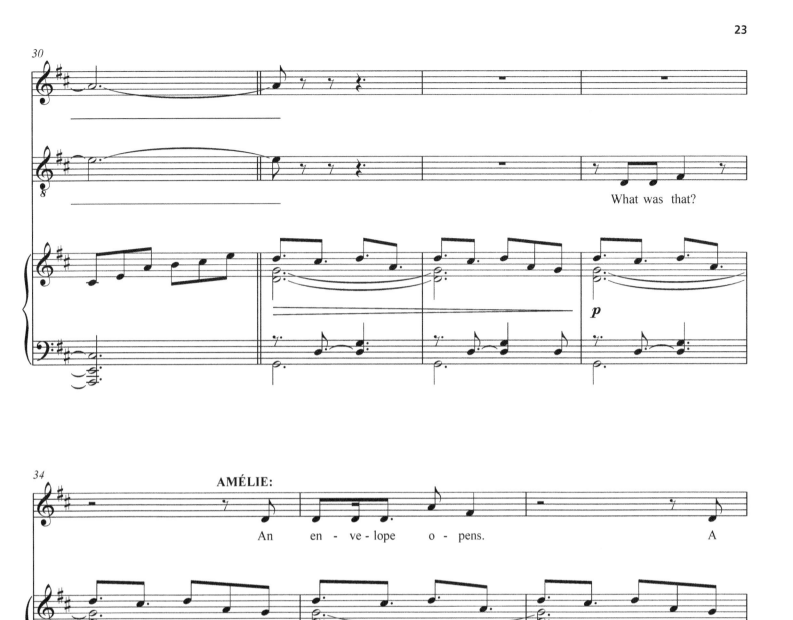

What was that?

AMÉLIE:

An en - ve - lope o - pens. A

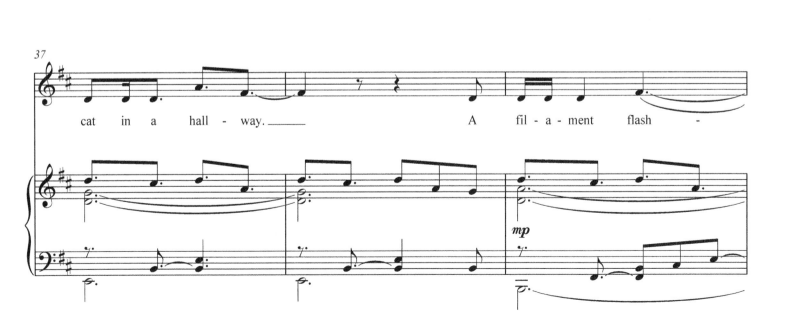

cat in a hall - way._____ A fil - a - ment flash -

es. Flick-ers and dies. And there goes a hat, __

cresc.

AMÉLIE:

thrown in the air. __

BLIND BEGGAR:

thrown in the air. __

mf

Thrown in the air! _____ I can feel ev - 'ry

Thrown in the air! _____ I can feel ev - 'ry

ff

f

We end up o - pen wide __

dim.

mp

AMÉLIE:

Here where the bus - ses stop, you can find a

ki - osk un - der sta - ples and glue.

Now the bar - ber shop, now the laun - dro - mat, now we're at the met - ro, a -

GOODBYE AMÉLIE

Lyrics by NATHAN TYSEN and DANIEL MESSÉ
Music by DANIEL MESSÉ

beats me girl, why you had to bid this plan - et a - dieu.

Let me be _____ the first to say _____ "Mer - ci _____ girl." _____ That means

"Thank _____ you." We're an o - cean of row - boats you de - cid - ed to save. _____ Lift - ing

us to the shore - line like a wave. When your harp and your ha - lo hit

♩ = 81

harp and your ha - lo hit the sky, look down, __
hit the sky,
hit the sky,

E.J.:

__ we'll be wav - ing good - bye. _____

CHOIR: *(men 8vb)*

Oh where will we go?__ Oh who will ap - pease __ us? You're nic - er than O -

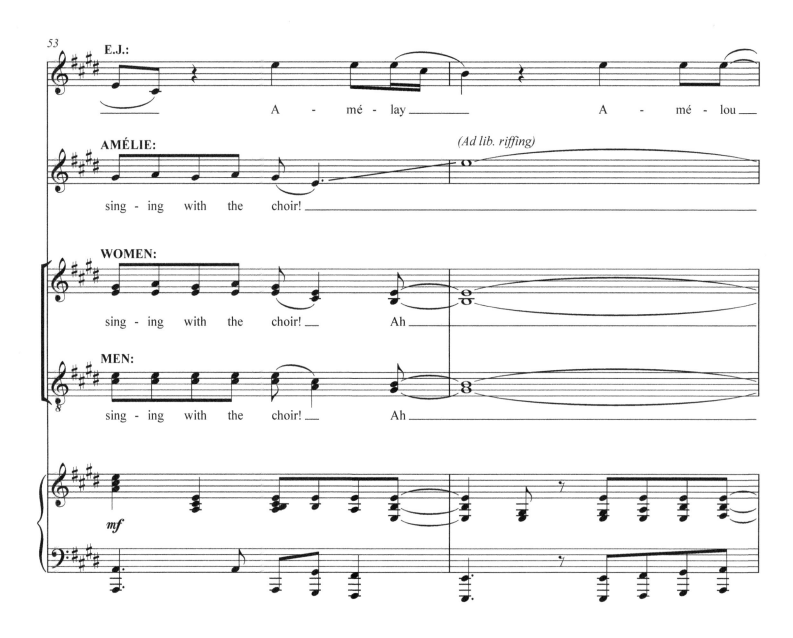

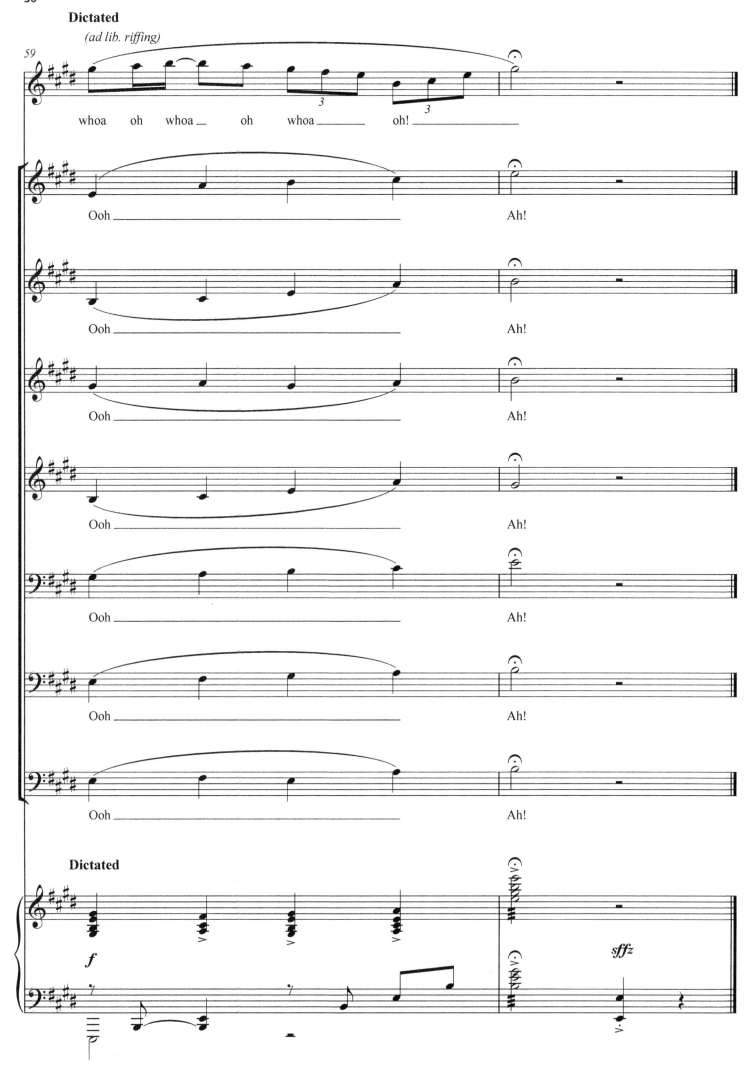

WHEN THE BOOTH GOES BRIGHT

Lyrics by NATHAN TYSEN and DANIEL MESSÉ
Music by DANIEL MESSÉ

you were. There's your trip a - broad. There's your fa - ther's smile. There's the

face of God. There is ev' - ry - thing that you were ___ and you still want to be. ___

What do you see ___

straight 16ths

when the booth ___ goes bright?

(flash)   *(flash)*

swung 16ths

SISTER'S PICKLE

Lyrics by NATHAN TYSEN and DANIEL MESSÉ
Music by DANIEL MESSÉ

58

Sees something intriguing/disturbing.

wow! _____

I take a step to get

61

out, but my feet for - get how. _____

64

Now it's me. Just

67

me a - gainst the door This is - n't what I thought,

al - though I think I want____ some more.

But not right now, now I need____ to go.

I'm not fin - ished with the boy, I mean the *book*.

So I will hold him— hold *it* 'til to - mor - row.

p

HALFWAY

Lyrics by NATHAN TYSEN and DANIEL MESSÉ
Music by DANIEL MESSÉ

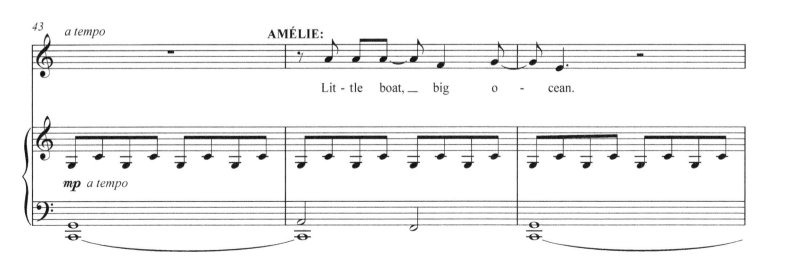

- cean _____ with al - ways half - way to go. _____

- cean _____ with al - ways half - way to go. _____

To go! _____

To go! _____

THIN AIR

Lyrics by NATHAN TYSEN and DANIEL MESSÉ
Music by DANIEL MESSÉ

THE LATE NINO QUINCAMPOIX

Lyrics by NATHAN TYSEN and DANIEL MESSÉ
Music by DANIEL MESSÉ

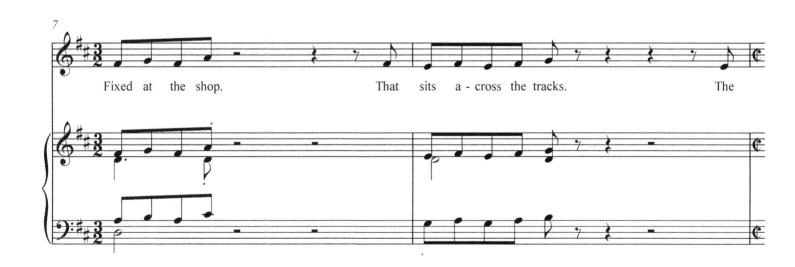

A BETTER HAIRCUT

Lyrics by NATHAN TYSEN and DANIEL MESSÉ
Music by DANIEL MESSÉ

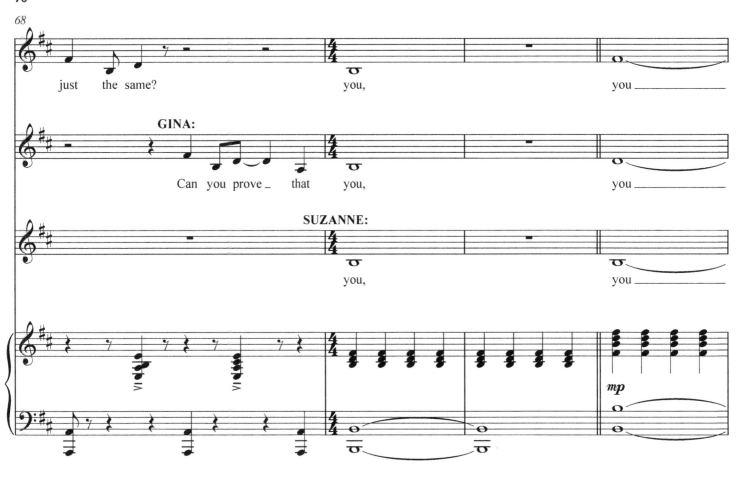

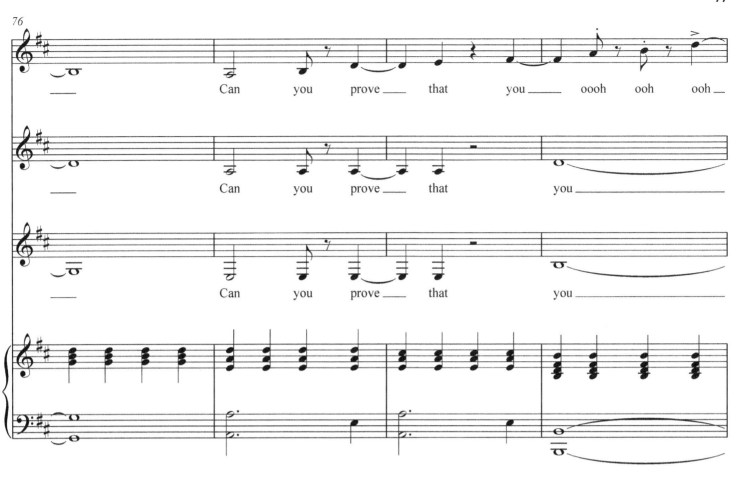

Can you prove ___ that you ___ oooh ooh ooh ___

Can you prove ___ that you ___

Can you prove ___ that you ___

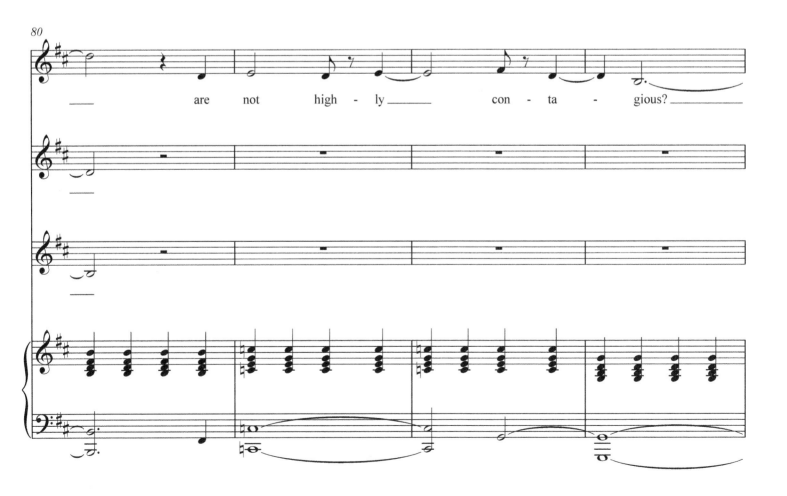

are not high - ly ___ con - ta - gious? ___

84

Oh yes. Love is just an - oth - er

Oh yes.

Oh yes.

88 GEORGETTE:

di - ag - no - sis, like bac - te - ri - al va - gi - no - sis

91

GEORGETTE:

to ev - 'ry thing that you trans - mit - ted.

GINA:

Once you're in it you're com - mit - ted

SUZANNE:

Once you're in it you're com - mit - ted

ALL 3 WAITRESSES:
If you're gon-na be the guy to date her, give her space and don't suf-fo-cate _ her. You might make 'em stop and stare, _ but you could use a bet-ter hair - cut.

(ad lib)
GEORGETTE:
Love is just an-oth-er di-ag-no-sis like

GINA & SUZANNE:
You _ might be a chick-en pox, swine flu, strep-to-coc-cus, walk-ing pneu - mo - nia, mumps, her-lov - er for _ the ag - es, _

un - der - stand___ she may not e - ven feel the same.___ I

love her and I don't know her name.

Tempo I

WAITRESSES:

All the whi - le whi - le

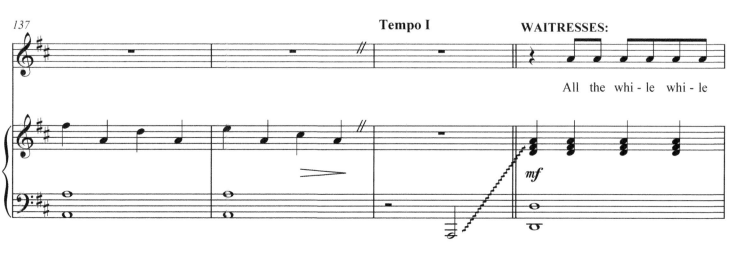

STAY

Lyrics by NATHAN TYSEN and DANIEL MESSÉ
Music by DANIEL MESSÉ

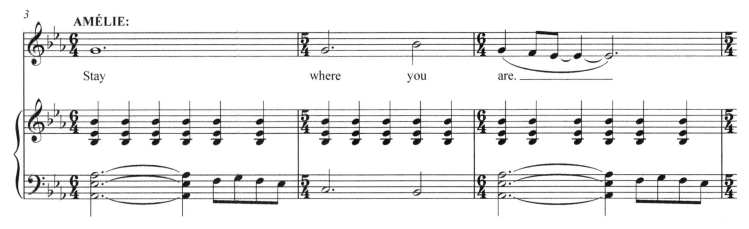

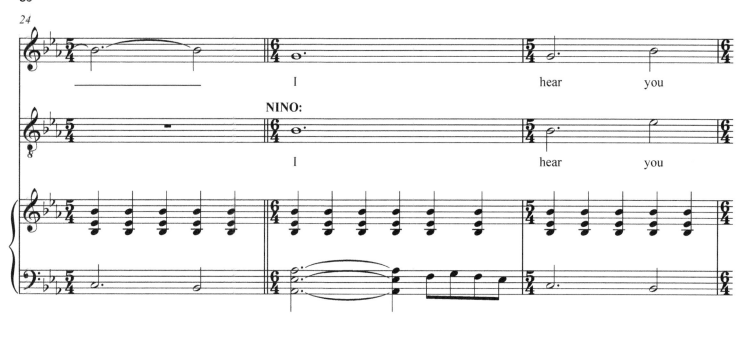

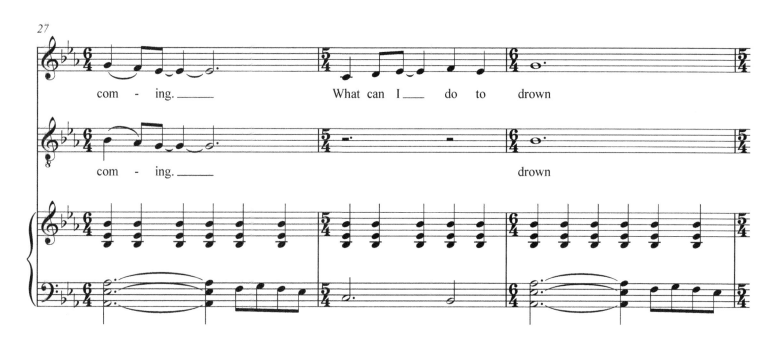

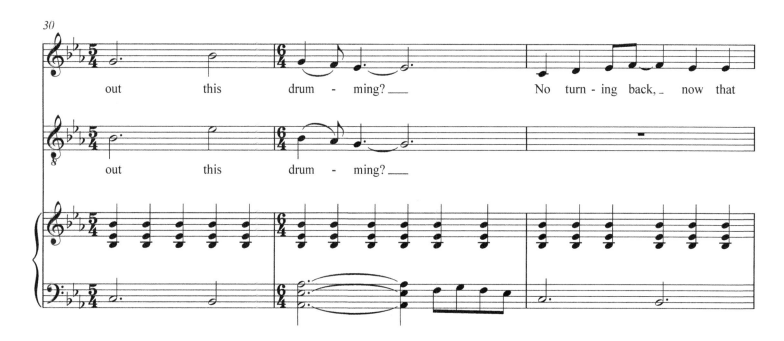

WHERE DO WE GO FROM HERE

Lyrics by NATHAN TYSEN and DANIEL MESSÉ
Music by DANIEL MESSÉ

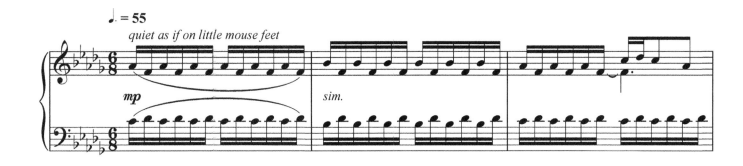

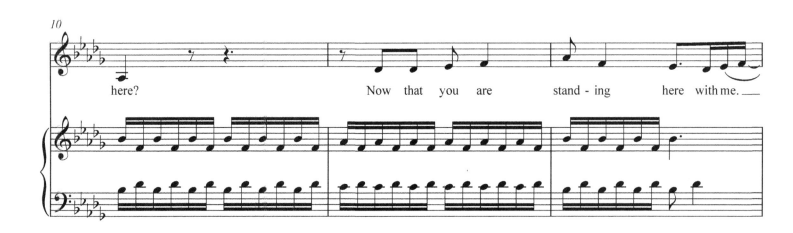

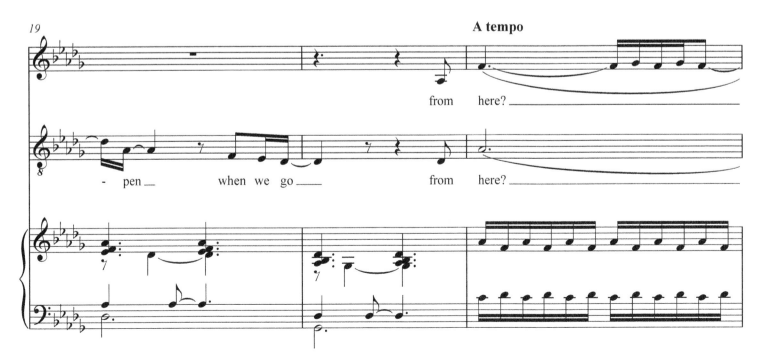

-pens, here we go.___ What's gon-na hap - pen? And where do we

-pens, What's gon-na hap - pen? And where do we

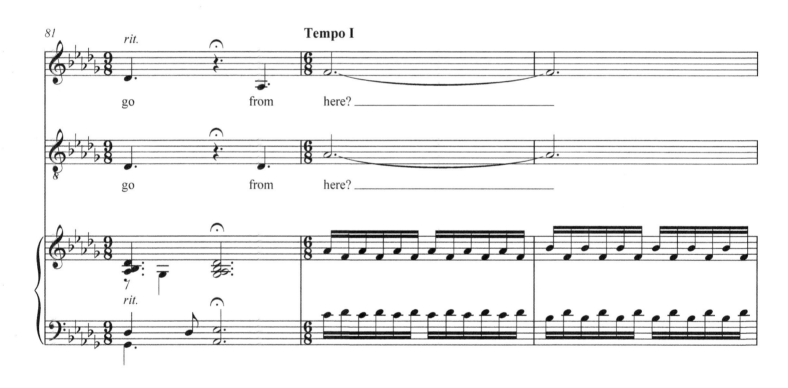

rit. **Tempo I**

go from here?_____

go from here?_____

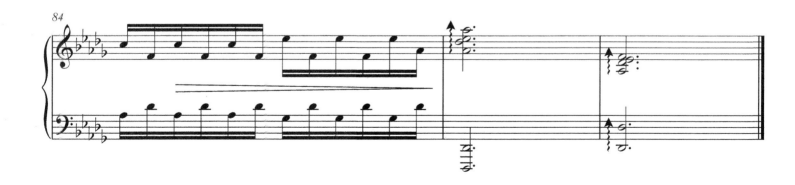